STONE UNIVERSE

To Lydia and David

Love and Best Wishes

Carol

Mood and landscape
Defining times of peace
When even our own noise
Stills
For a moment.

STONE UNIVERSE

Carol Ballenger

Poetry by John Powls

HALSGROVE

This book is dedicated to my Arts Live collaborators
Graham, John and Sam.

First published in Great Britain in 2001

ISBN 1 84114 134 8

British Library Cataloguing-in-Publication Data
A CIP record for this title is available from the British Library

HALSGROVE
Halsgrove House
Lower Moor Way
Tiverton, Devon EX16 6SS
Tel: 01884 243242
Fax: 01884 243325
email sales@halsgrove.com
website www.halsgrove.com

Printed and bound in Italy by Centro Grafico Ambrosiano, Milan

Foreword

To see a World in a Grain of Sand
And a Heaven in a Wild Flower,
Hold Infinity in the palm of your hand
And Eternity in an hour.'

Auguries of Innocence

These much quoted words of William Blake (1757–827) convey with clarity and simplicity the depth of field that surrounds our lives. Things can be seen in such ways with detailed knowledge or explanation, but there are times when comprehension is not needed and when to just look is enough. The visual and conceptual images in *Stone Universe* portray aspects of Dartmoor at their *face value* and through these individual worlds we can glean a collective universe.

When looking at a map, or travelling in a car, Dartmoor can seem small, usually too small to conjure up images of infinity and eternity. But stand on Fur Tor, crouch at boulder-moss level in Holne Woods, be immersed in birdsong on Hameldown, sense the flow of the East Dart River, feel the frailty of growan, sit alongside Down Tor stone row in failing light and contemplate. All such experiences provide opportunities for each of us, through a sense of place and time, to look beyond. Photographic and word imagery can also provide such opportunities. For example, when viewing the panoramas in this publication our horizons are unusually expanded not only *within* the elongated frame but also outside these confines – we might be led to ask what does lie beyond the edge of things?

The following pages are also an evocation of stone and its surfaces. There is an elemental beauty here, but *Stone Universe* also depicts the way in which nature and people influence the interface. This is not a universe where there are no smells, no tastes, no sense of touch, no vision and only silences. In many of these images life is apparent, but sometimes it is suggested, subtle, frozen, or vestigial and we are aware that life begins and leads somewhere.

Through these images, even though only representing moments in time, we can sense movement and change – here are cloud shifts, clitter strewn slopes, rearranged moorstone, autumn berries, river-borne leaves, branches caught in eddies, wind-blown winter grasses, snow, ice, phases of the day and the moon, shadows, nature's patterns and textures, ephemeral translucencies and juxtapositions; here are the delicate and the strong, the fading colour, the prostrate, the bent, the vertical, the interlaced and the broken.

2001 marked the fiftieth anniversary of the designation of Dartmoor as a National Park. But fifty years is just a blip in the aeons that have passed in this stone universe. We are finding out more and more about what has occurred in the past and each of us in some way influences the present; what lies in the future, beyond *our* tomorrows, what lies under the surface of things, we can only surmise.

Carol Ballenger and John Powls are two of a recent, developing and exciting genre of artists to interpret Dartmoor and their relationships with it. Whether watching, stalking, feeling, and imagining, and whether working with stone, wood, film, paints and other materials, or through words, music and other forms, important new voices speaking of Dartmoor, its life, its qualities, and our personal responses to them, are emerging.

John W H Weir
Dartmoor National Park Authority

Listen to the land

Fallen cold, petals
Sky flowers of slow winter
White scent dressing stones.

Vixen Tor

STONE UNIVERSE

Here, where the granite intruder
Makes his point
And matters are brought to a head,
Ancient rocks are strewn
With careless intent;
Like uncut gems,
Seamed from a rich vein,
Spread on the merchant's cloth.
They are constellations
In a stone universe
On a green firmament.
Each has its starburst lichen
Spread supernova red, yellow
And dark as the blackest hole
On the cold, dense medium.
Expanding still, so fast
Yet too slow to see.
With only the memory
Of its molten birth,
Which exploding made
Their order from chaos.
The living earth.

Merrivale Menhir

Introduction

For many years landscape has been an important part of my life. As a child I lived in the foothills of the Appalachian Mountains in the USA and soon developed an affinity with the surrounding countryside. I also vividly remember a visit to Dartmoor as a seven year old, having returned to my native Devon for a holiday with my family. Here was a magic and mysterious place, shrouded with mists and steeped in legends, which haunted my memories for years.

Later I worked in London as a professional violinist during which time I became interested in photography. I returned to Devon in 1980 and began photographing various subjects, soon being drawn to work in the landscape and to Dartmoor in particular.

Hound Tor

Circle in snow, Haytor Down

Inspired by the paintings of the celebrated Dartmoor artist F. J. Widgery, I photographed the granite landmarks of tors, standing stones, crosses and bridges. Stone and its historical significance define this upland landscape. The wooded valleys on the lower slopes, carved out by gushing boulder-strewn rivers, lead to lower farmlands. On the high open moor, skies can be enormous and often dramatic, followed by low clouds which envelop the tors. Here silence is punctuated by the wind and rain, and on a fine day by lark song and the mew of buzzards.

Representing a place that over the years humans have endeavoured to observe, tame and conserve, the photographs I made became my first body of work, *Dartmoor Dreams*, from which the black and white images in this book were selected. The wilderness portrayed here only exists in our minds, for the land has been constantly reshaped since people began clearing trees from large areas of Dartmoor some eight

Merrivale double stone row

River Avon

thousand years ago. However the special qualities of this landscape remain.

The colour photographs in this book celebrate details of rock, ice, water, air, wood and vegetation. I spent many hours walking, looking, considering and sometimes photographing the landscape. In such a place contact with earth and rock seems to slow down perceptions of time. These photographs are about more than fragments of nature that interest me. They are meditations on the landscape – observations distilled through the camera lens. As well as documenting the world, photographs can reflect qualities of ourselves and our relationship to what is photographed – qualities of which we might have previously been unaware.

The images are also about colour. As a musician I have always been interested in tonal 'colours', how they influence our thinking and how they can be combined for aesthetic effect. Throughout history artists and scientists, including

River Dart

Haytor from Smallacombe Rocks

Goethe and Kandinsky, have expounded various colour theories, associating colours with feelings and music. I have used colour as one would use tonal colour in music – as an element of expression in its own right and to emphasise the character of the image.

The American naturalist Henry David Thoreau observed, 'How much of beauty – colour, as well as form – on which our eyes daily rest goes unperceived by us. There is just as much beauty visible to us in the landscape as we are prepared to appreciate – not a grain more'.[1] The images are part of that diverse universe, placed in context by the inclusion of the six panoramas.

This work has been inspired by the poetry of John Powls to whom I am indebted for the use of his poems. The various sections of the book are introduced by text which mirrors the mood of the photographs that follow. Much of the text is new and specially written for the project, the collaboration often consisting of a spiral of

Moor near East Dart Falls

The Touchstone, Rundlestone Crest

Inspiring
This stone touching
Open moor and sky
Granite land mark
Raised to stand for
All times as one time;
Now, then and ever
In love and beauty
Our story is a book
Always open
At the centre
Half of experiences
Half of un-named hopes.

The Touchstone is the first standing stone to be raised on Dartmoor for several thousand years. It has been inscribed with one of John Powls' poems and erected to celebrate the millennium.

River Avon

inspiration from images to text to images and so on.

The photographer Ansel Adams once said, 'I am glad that the artist can move through the wilderness taking nothing from its inexhaustible spirit and bring his vision-modulated fragments to all who come to see'.[2] These photographs are not literal descriptions. They are representations of the spirit and magic of Dartmoor – fragments of the 'Stone Universe'.

Carol Ballenger

[1] Henry David Thoreau, *Selections from the Journals*, Dover Publications, 1955

[2] Ansel Adams, *Yosemite and the Range of Light*, Little, Brown & Company, 1979

Your menhir stone is raised
Where time is measured in seasons
And the passage of sun and moon.

STONE UNIVERSE

perfect dark, flawless
thwarted voice, poignant silence
hear the stone dreaming.

Watch the January sky
Slide indifferent,
Slowly down
Chromatic scales.
Reduce the tones
To glacier blue and
A long and sonorous
Umbral charcoal.

Ocean tree;
Sail by
Wind whipped
Sail
Leaf flotilla.

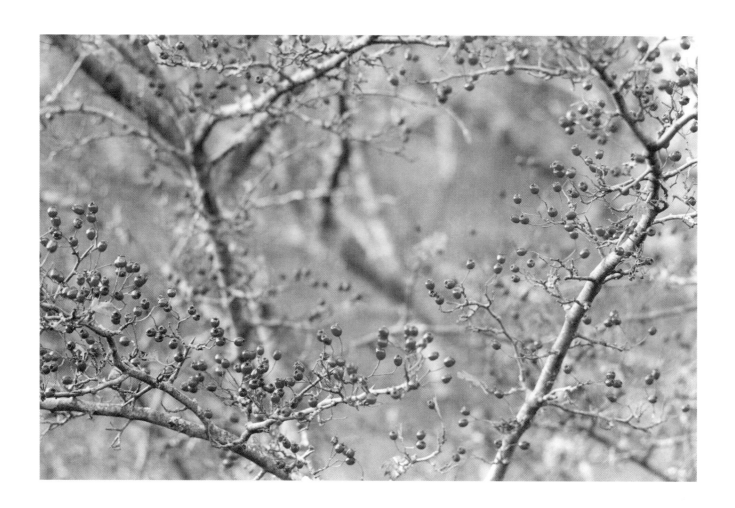

Fate undertows
Crash ecstatic
Where the pulse wave breaks
Dark and supple, surging
Over submerged rock.

Gatherer,
Land taker, land maker.
Decreating, recreating,
Inexorable leveller
Spoken of as being,
Life giver, life taker.
So turns the earth.

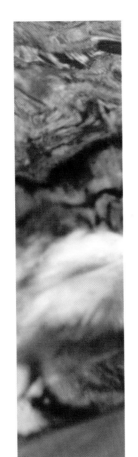
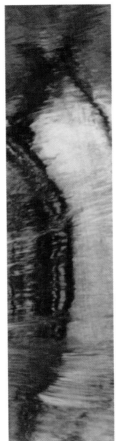

rainbow
palette of colours
straight from the tube transient
breath mist on glass sky.

Clearing sky,
Soft gaze
Faithful sun
Lights on
Moment
Of stillness
And silence.

Wait for breath
Of inspiration
To sweep the air.

The vital words
Of landscape
Echo round
The bare walls
Of time.

74

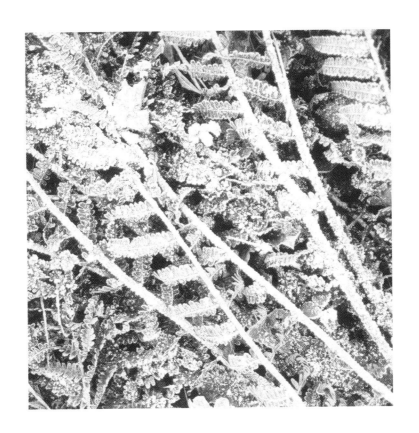

moment after shot
quiet as a photograph
nature held its breath.

Dewed grass drizzled with brown
And sodden leaves, fire damped.
Blackberry eyed squirrel and crow
Dip the teeming shallows
For acorn, hip and fallen fruit.

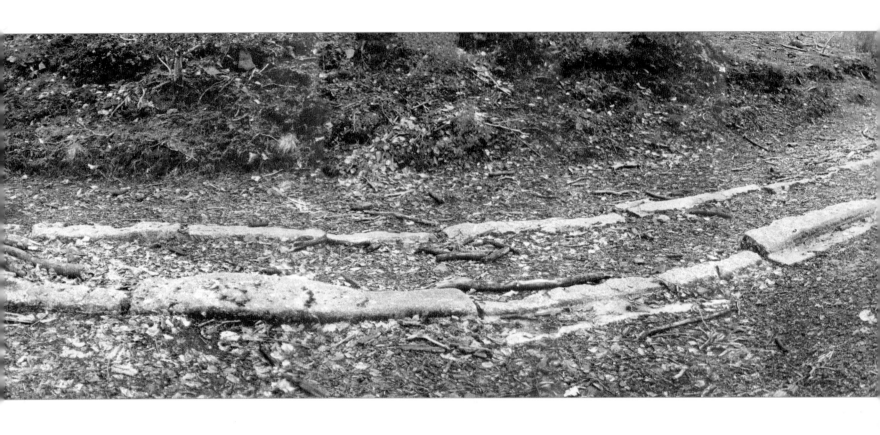

The sky is a delicate
Watercolour grey.
I watch hushed rain
Drop
Through the fading light
To gently startle
The chestnut leaves
From their reflecting
On green's transaction
With red and brown.

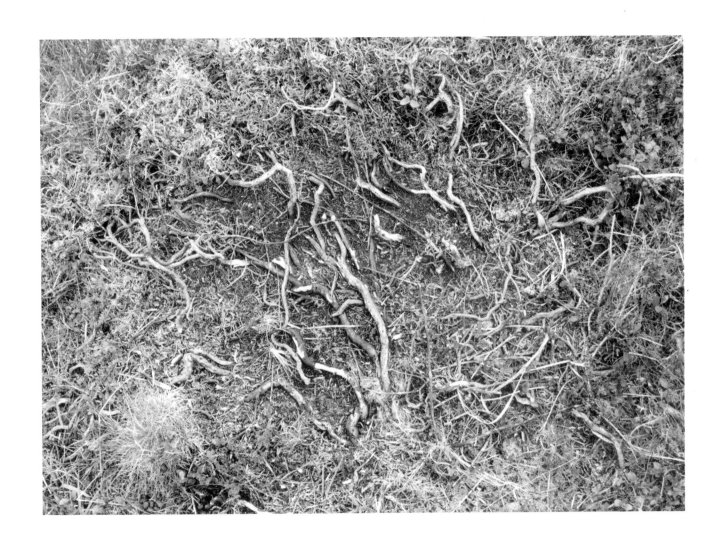

The passion
Summer storm
Spent;
In that time
All the beauty
Of the world.

Art
Of floating worlds
Assembled elements,
Nature given;
Simplicity, order, beauty…

such fragrance; where from?
stone tree or distant meadow
first scent of summer.

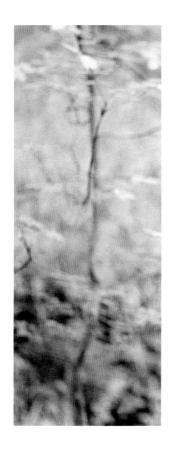 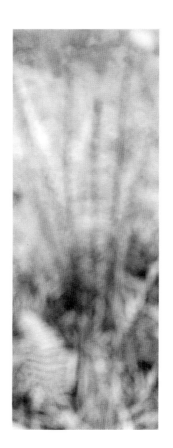 

Listen to the land.

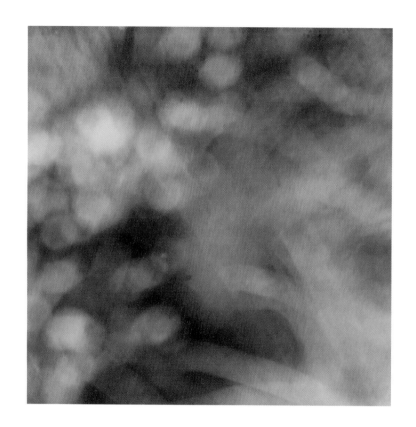

List of Photographs

Acknowledgements

I would like to thank the following for their encouragement and support of this project:

John Weir and the Dartmoor National Park Authority
Bob Butler, David Drake and South West Arts
Simon Butler, Karen Binaccioni and Halsgrove Publishing
Stephen Pettit-Smith, Kelly Ryan and Exeter Health Care Arts
Louise Ingle and the First Western National Bus Company
Doff Pollard and Teignbridge District Council
William Bishop
Kathy Downton
Helena Kovacs

my *Arts Live* collaborators John Powls and Sam Richards
and particularly Graham Hodgson for his technical support, enthusiasm and help with sequencing the photographs.

John Powls – Having written poetry for over 25 years John Powls' work has been published extensively in poetry journals, anthologies and newspapers. He has broadcast his work on radio and television and is a regular performer at major festivals and other poetry venues. A collection of his poems titled *Galerie d'Amour* was published in 1998. To celebrate the new millennium a menhir stone, 'The Touchstone', inscribed with one of his poems was raised at Rundlestone Crest, Dartmoor.

'Red Comet fuelled' J.P.

This publication is supported by the South West Arts Regional Lottery Programme, Year of the Artist, Dartmoor National Park Authority and Teignbridge District Council.

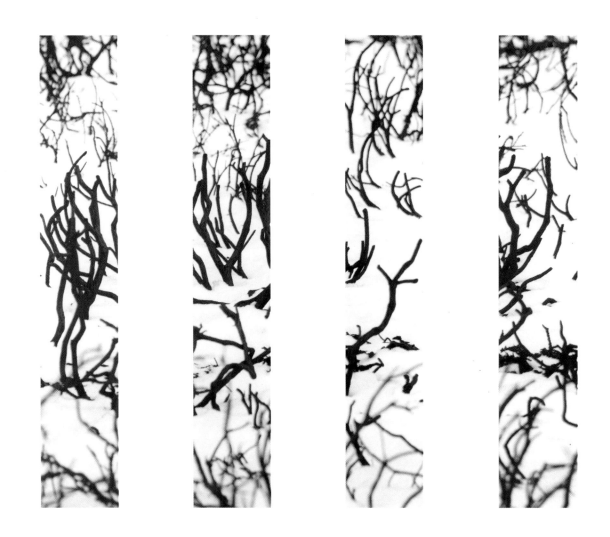